MUSIC
from
APARTMENT
8

voice stay in your heart.

Nancy Fajman

Also by John Stone

Music FROM Apartment 8

New and Selected Poems

· John Stone ·

LOUISIANA STATE UNIVERSITY PRESS

BATON ROUGE

2004

Designer: Andrew Shurtz
Typeface: Minion
Printer and binder: Thomson-Shore, Inc.

Library of Congress Cataloging-in-Publication Data:
Stone, John, 1936–
Music from apartment 8 : new and selected poems / John Stone.
p. cm.
ISBN 0-8071-2953-4 (cloth : alk. paper) —
ISBN 0-8071-2954-2 (pbk. : alk. paper)
I. Title: Music from apartment eight. II. Title.
PS3569.T6413M87 2004
811'.54—dc22
2003017430

Poems herein have been selected from *In All This Rain* (Louisiana State
University Press, 1980), copyright © 1980 by John Stone; *Renaming the
Streets* (Louisiana State University Press, 1985), copyright © 1985 by John
Stone; *The Smell of Matches* (Louisiana State University Press, 1972), copy-
right © 1972 by John Stone; *Where Water Begins* (Louisiana State
University Press, 1998), copyright © 1986, 1987, 1990, 1992, 1995, 1996, 1997,
1998 by John Stone. Poems appearing in book form for the first time here
were originally published in *Denver Quarterly:* "Back through Time"; *Five
Points:* "Tuesday at the Assisted Care Home," "Processional: A Follow-Up";
Georgia Review: "Caduceus," "Imagine with Me Now the Final Room"; and
Southern Review: "Visitation," "Baalbek."

Contents

The Smell of Matches (1972)

In All This Rain (1980)

Renaming the Streets (1985)

Where Water Begins (1998)

· New Poems ·

Serenity Gardens

for PAULINE M. STONE

~

"... she enters the poems as the whole mystery a mother is."
—SEAMUS HEANEY

Tuesday at the Assisted Care Home

I am taking in the shade, she the sun.
Together we are planning whole new lives.
Then suddenly the spelling bee group from
inside Serenity Gardens is upon us. They move

outside *en masse:* six women and one man.
She and I are surrounded and outnumbered.
So we join in, I to listen, she to spell. I'd wager
she is the oldest of this group. The spelling bee begins.

At first all the "P" words come her way: she spells
with relish each in turn, easily mowing them down:
paisley   preference   parsonage   palisade
This woman is my only mother, now 93,

who loves to sit in the sun, smiling out from under
her great straw hat in lighting by Vermeer.
If she is not, this morning, the oldest here,
clearly she is the most beautiful.

Then the spelling rules change: Now she is
to pick a word beginning with the letter "B"
then spell it. She ponders. BLASPHEME, she says
finally, spelling: B-L-A-S-P-H-E-M-E—BLASPHEME.

Everyone is suitably impressed, you might say
even startled. The woman next to me says
in an unnecessary *sotto voce,* Your mother
is a great speller, but where do you reckon

did she come up with a word like that?
I have no idea, I reply, no idea. After popsicles,
the party's over. The group disperses slowly
with chair and cane. Not a blasphemer

among them as far as I can tell. Then she and I
are again alone together, both of us
now brightly under the sun in its highest rising.
Under her great straw hat in this lighting by Vermeer

she stretches in the heat. I speak to her dozing eyes
deep in brim-shadow: You look a lot like
Katherine Hepburn in that hat—in *The African Queen*—
remember? Her eyelids flicker open:

You can say THAT again!
And with a regal smile all her own, still aiming
at a whole new life, she settles back
and gathers unto herself

the sun

and her son.

Frances

Saturday afternoon at Serenity Gardens. As is their wont,
the ladies (mostly) are having wine and cheese

by the piano in the parlor. I'm taking some cheddar
and crackers for my mother when the spry and spiffy

woman seated along the wall motions to me: I go to
her and bend: Her hair is bouffant, her white suit

immaculate with beaded blouse. "You're going to get fat,"
she says, eyeing my plate and me, "if you eat all that."

It's not for me, I say—it's for my mother, who can stand
the pounds. I introduce myself as Polly's son. Her name is Frances.

You enjoying the party? I ask. "Yes," says Frances,
beaming. "Did you know I'll be 100 years old next July 25?"

*No, I didn't know that. You'll need to have a big
party then, to celebrate.* "Oh, don't you see?" she says.

"I've been having lots of parties all along!
That's why I'm going to be 100 years old next July!"

Visitation

December 2001

At Serenity Gardens, winter
has surrounded us. My mother's room
is way too warm for me,

just right for her—with an extra sweater.
Outside, this uneasy year, her 93rd,
lurches through December.

She is surely serene in this place,
thanks to whatever goodness;
queen of the electronic piano.

Among my chief duties now
I have become her human calendar,
a stay against time, her reach for the past.

Each visit, we review the years.
We sit and we talk, fragile mother,
absent-minded son.

This afternoon, I assemble for her
some semblance of my long-dead
father, the only husband she had.

I tell her his story.
We study his photograph.
Do you remember him, I ask?

She looks again.
No, she answers, softly. *No.*
But isn't he good looking!

She smiles. I chuckle.
In the gathering dark,
we cry a bit together:

I for what she has forgotten,
she for what I remember.

Noon, Thursday

I dropped in
on my mother
dazzling in her yellow sweater
having lunch.

I sat down
at her table.
I'd seen her
two days ago

but this time
I startled her
I think—too early
in the week

for another visit.
*You just appeared
out of nowhere!*
she said

then asked me, smiling:
*What have you been doing
all these years?*
I didn't know what to say.

It's the very
same question
I've been asking myself.

Patriot at the Pianoforte

Just after Mums entered Serenity Gardens
we took her to Sears to buy some eyeglasses.
On the way to Optometry, though, we got waylaid
by the electronic pianos.

What a Christmas present that would be!
said my brother—I agreed, the Hungarian Rhapsody
she raised us on coming to mind. Let's not forget,
she kept saying, impatient in her wheelchair,

Let's not forget what we came here for!
But my brother and I were already note-besotted,
as we tickled and arpeggioed the keys of
the Yamahas and Casios.

We lurched from the full-throated organ
to the elegant sounds of the baby grand
then on to Scott Joplin, who roused at
the touch of a button.

We like this piano, we told the clerk,
We'll be back! We wheeled on over, then,
happy as if we had good sense, to get the classiest
bifocals we could find. We doubled back for the piano.

That evening, we struggled to put Tab A into Slot A
and so on to let the music out. The piano worked first time
like the dream that Mums, for that day, was already
slowly entering. And we all slept then,

dancing and ragging.

        ∾

Next morning when Mums woke up in her room,
her eyes were startled open by the sleek black shape
in the corner, its white teeth and blinking lights
menacing, waiting for music.

I took one look at that thing this morning, she said,
and almost jumped outta my skin. I didn't remember
it being here when I went to sleep, she smiled.
But this is the best toy I've had in a long time,

she said, revving up her fingers. And she called
that piano into service all the way from her family home
in Prosper, Texas, which didn't, all the way
to her corner of Serenity Gardens, which,

belatedly, was beginning to rock.

⁓

She took to this piano as we hoped she might:
fingers do not forget the chromatic scales
any more than feet the leaning bicycle.
She tamed the keyboard, calling all those obedient

electrons to order, winter to spring, spring to summer,
softening the fall of fall. She especially loved to play
"America the Beautiful." She played it to celebrate
every visit we made to see her: Christmas, New Year's,

Valentine's Day, Easter, the summer solstice, whenever
any given day seemed in need of a tune.
We'd never known the song even had four verses
but we learned them all in self-defense.

And whatever grace might be seemed to smile down
on the slight, white-sweatered woman
making so much music in Apartment 8.
We clasped shoulders and sang the words,

learning by heart what she taught by hand.
And purple mountains' majesties rose
above the fruited plain. And all was well
along Medlock Road, to which the universe

was paying no attention.

~

All this happened before the Old Testament
became overnight the New, before Lamentations
became the book of Revelation
before September 11, 2001

before the two planes found the twin towers
napping in the New York morning sun
And the rest of the world caught suddenly
and forever up with her.

We have never told her about what happened
beyond Serenity Gardens. Her merciful world
is little changed. Her notes roll upward in a mighty
fugue toward the holes in heaven.

And she still plays.

And we still sing.

~

Sunday afternoon in the hospital. The patient sleeps fitfully. I sit by her
bed, my head resting on the rail. From time to time, she rises through the
gauze of sleep, rouses through the chloroform of fatigue and moans. The
past 48 hours—tests and more tests—have been hard for both of us. Now,
in my dozing brain, I am aware of a recurring pattern to her moans: for
several minutes, she rests quietly, then begins again, softly at first, then
louder. There is a diamond shape to her pain: *crescendo,* then *decrescendo.*
It is the old nemesis I hoped not to see: biliary colic. I know already that
she has pancreatitis and a bag full of gall stones. I have just been witness as
she passed another stone. The matter is settled. This 94 year old woman,
this mother full of misery, will have to have surgery.

After Surgery

I think perhaps this woman is my child.
—JOHN CIARDI

Above Serenity Gardens
the sun is a hot-bright disk,
moon-high, yellow-white,
on crayon-blue paper.

My mother and I are on the deck,
rambling in childhood, tumbling
in the sieve of memory.

Three weeks after her surgery
she is still weak as water,
brittle with osteoporosis, a trooper.
She leans her head back against
the wheelchair; her straw hat
tips forward over her face.

Blue-eyed, hatless, I improvise
against sunburn, folding
the newspaper that way and this
to make a three-cornered hat:
it takes shape in my hands
like a gift from Napoleon.

Now we are both hooded,
a pair of senior goblins
ready for Halloween—
we nap in a nest of pumpkins
and corn stalks. Our heads loll.

Suddenly, looming out of the blue
sky, the physical therapist appears,
rousing us from our reverie
with a loud voice:

"Whoa!" she says,
"What do we have here?"

I turn my hooded eyes toward her,
tip my newspaper hat.

The therapist smiles benignly—
but we are not fooled.

We know why she has come:
to stretch my mother's tight quads,
to lengthen her thin contracted hamstrings
in a session worthy of the rack.

She means business—
and as we know from her first visit
pain is part of her business.

She wants my mother
in her clutches, three times a week,
as scheduled.

Imagine her surprise, then,
when my mother and I rise
from the flight deck of Serenity Gardens,
moving aloft together, in a dream
of a winged escape from prison.

We are flying together,
flapping our wings, looping
through the startled sky.

We circle above the therapist,
now a tiny dot, who will have to wait
for her appointment.

We are tempted, like Icarus,
like all children, to fly
straight for the sun.

But what matters most now
is to soar
into the blue wild yonder
on the bird bones of osteoporosis
riding high and well

beyond her reaches.

Processional: A Follow-Up

After daily sessions on the rack
my mother rises from her bed to walk.

Down the hall we make a kind of train:
my mother's first, the engine and the brain.

Next the therapist in single file
urges my mother's feet. All the while

I wheel the empty chair behind them both,
an earnest rear guard, tucked up close,

lest the lady general need to take,
in the sweep of battle, a sudden seat. We make

a left and lurch into the dining hall,
catching Keith and Yolanda resetting all

the tenants' places for lunch. Smiling then,
they begin to clap—and the house joins in

to form a mighty circle of applause
for my mother, who has broken all the laws,

who seemed just now to walk on water—or wine,
or, for that matter, air. And she sits down to dine.

Mosaics:
Reflections from the Middle East

for Max Miller, *for* Pat Pattillo

Baalbek

At the Temple of Bacchus
in the white heat of noon
a young woman

her sunglasses gleaming
in her hair
glamorous vision in white

pants and sweater
perches on a toppled
Romanesque column

talking animatedly
on her cellular
phone

staying in close
and daily touch
with all the ages

Jerash: Potsherds

All morning
in only the shade of hats,
we learn what to look for

beyond the Ionic columns:
pottery shards
the parallel lines

of the whirling pots
the lost kisses
of their fluted lips.

What may we guess
from this?
That these folks

were often hungry
hereabouts: evidence
of this lingers

as well as the fact that
they had to work to cook
and eat.

And at least
some of them
were fumblefingers.

Spiritual

Go down, Moses.
Way down in Egypt land.
Tell old Pharaoh:
Let my people go.

My father
used to sing that refrain
in the shower

in Jackson
Mississippi
in 1954.

The year he finally
got out of Egypt
he was 45 years old.

He died before
coronary care
Before the defibrillator

Before lidocaine
monitors
Before intensive care

nurses.
They put him in
an oxygen tent

They made the diagnosis
just for show
They hoped the best for him.

We let him go.

Back through Time

Like the plague doctor
dispensing the magic
I move among the victims:

They open. They swallow.

Like him, I deal only
with the here and now, the stomach's
gripe, the blinding nausea

that may come before or follow.

It is just as though
I too were wearing
the full-length leather gown

of medieval power

but minus the honorable gloves,
the bird hat, its coned nose
filled with antiseptic

to protect me now, of course,

but especially at the hour.

Mount Sinai: Chasing the Sun

Dark. Dark coffee, privately. Each of us alone
in the dark of being a self. It's 1 A.M.
The whole sensible world is asleep.
Our bus shudders half a mile and slows:

its doors wheeze open on the immensity
of Mount Sinai above St. Catherine's Monastery.
Already, camels are kneeling in the courtyard
like islands surfaced from the sand.

I throw my right leg clumsily over my assigned
hump. I hold on: Up, Forward, Reverse, a deep dip
and curtsy. My camel and I rise into starlight.
Our caravan stretches out single-file toward

the distant commandments and the known sun.
I lean back in the darkness, try to get comfortable
on the thin blanket atop my perch. Too soon,
the camel stops, kneels with a jolt. I slip to the sand,

deftly it seems to me. My flashlight picks out
the jagged footholds ahead. This will not be easy.
I climb. A thousand steps later, it's clear I'm not
keeping up: young voices, German, Italian, scurry by.

On the next plateau, I almost stumble over
two struggling friends. One has fallen.
Her bleeding knee is enough to stop me: it doesn't take much.
I will be her doctor for a while, a Samaritan on Mount Sinai.

We have not reached the summit, I know.
But I also know I am 62 years old and on this mountain
closer than ever to 63. I tell my friends in front of God
and the prophets that I am stopping. The same sun

will be coming up here as higher up. I will wait for it.
We three sprawl, happily breathing. Then, above us,
a shooting star! Ten seconds of unearthed light curves by,
taking our surprised picture, time-lapse, through

the blue-black iris of sky. A sign, surely.
We wait and are rewarded: the sun is a slow dream
of daylight on a mountain I never thought to see this close.
There are oohs and aahs above and below me.

I point my camera at sunrise. Magically, then,
camels appear, headed down this time—
for a modest fee—all the blessèd way down
to the monastery and the bus.

Down turns out to be worse than *Up* in terms of camels:
I ride the same thin blanket aboard this swaying ship
in these ancient mountains. But each camel-clop
now thumps through my bony saddle—

and I must learn to endure
along my delicate straddle
the heavy ache
of my nomadic life.

Caduceus

I go with the student
in search of her health
in Amman   in Jordan:

Mary Sue is sick as a sheep.
The physician, Dr. Himmo,
I like instantly.

He's a gynecologist, I a cardiologist.
Between us, I figure we make just about
one general practitioner.

The bottle of intravenous fluids
is hung high. Turkish coffee, sweet and hot,
is brought for all of us, then sugary tea.

The saline drips like a water clock:
its syrup says Hello, brain,
muscles, skin, gut, Hello

lungs. And the great paddlewheel
of the heart kicks in
and the kidneys answer Amen.

Turns out Dr. Himmo
is a poet, too. He says a poem of his
in Arabic first, then English

a poem of first love long ago
about the always need to say good-bye:
"We will try to draw the picture

of sadness on the last page
of the book. We will try to make it
only a coincidence when we meet."

He writes the poem out for me in both
our languages. And as the fluid slows,
then stops, this coincidence of ours is over.

We thank Dr. Himmo for coffee, tea,
poems, electrolytes and make our way out.
Mary Sue leans on me

all the way down the elevator
all the way to the car:
One of the privileges

of the physician is to hold triumph,
love, and illness all together
in his arms.

But just before we leave
I remember to ask
my most important question

of Dr. Himmo:
How should I command healing
in his native tongue, in case

I need it for the rest of the trip?
Yeshfi, he says, smiling,
glowing behind his desk.

Yeshfi.

    for Mary Sue Brookshire

In Petra

After the hike
up to   down from   the highest
and most exhausted place

I am sleeping on the bench
outside the museum.
Preston is dozing nearby.

Comes now into our shade
the song of a nine-year-old Bedouin boy,
handsome as a prince:

Are you sleeping,
Are you sleeping,
Brother John? Brother John?

I know the song full well,
but not his smiling answer:
Can't you see I'm reading?

Can't you see I'm reading?
Ding dong ding.
Ding dong ding.

I tell him my name *is* John.
We sing the verse together.
I take his photograph.

I start to say how happy
I am this afternoon
to be a citizen of his kingdom.

But he has vanished into my sleep.

Before Sleep

What I remember is

white.
White houses
cars

head dress.
White.
And such shadows

as would have caused
Edward Hopper
to pitch a painting fit.

Also, before sleep, I decide:
Air conditioning
falls alike

on the just
and
the unjust.

Jerusalem: Bedtime

My roommate
Leonard
is writing

in his journal
keeping records
that will help me

in due course:
who did what
to whom and when

and in what archaeological
era. John, he says,
you go ahead

and take your shower
if you want to. I've got
some more notes to make here first.

Great, Leonard, I say,
if you're sure that's ok with you.
To which he replies,

That's fine!
I wanna do some pushups
before I take my shower, anyway.

Good man, Leonard,
I say, heading for the shower stall.
Do a few pushups for me, too,

won't you, old boy!

Hydra: Greece

From oak and pine to olive tree
I turn today to rock and sea
to island trawlers trailing foam—

to drachma now and next to dollar—
from nomad life to city scholar—
scroll and tablet turn to poem—

from veil and kaffir, camel, sand
from synagogue and caravan
from minaret to stately dome:

already, my heart is headed home.

First Night Back in Atlanta

At 4 A.M.
(11 A.M. Damascus time)
I woke and wandered

dazed
the halls of my home:
the floors were cool mosaic,

intricate and ancient.

Now, over coffee,
in daylight
I see my floors

for what they are:
plain, off-white,
carpeted.

And yet . . .

And yet . . .

Distances

for Mae Nelson

Looking for the Pal Theater

We have grown up as best we could.
—DEREK MAHON

Every Saturday along South Sycamore
my growing-up brother and I
floated like Two Stooges
in search of the Pal Theater
pop-eyed with lights.

Mostly, we couldn't find it.

Directionless as balloons,
helpless as Hansels dropping crumbs,
we circled, like lost Cub Scouts,
the tiny town of Palestine, Texas.

Maybe they *moved* the Pal, we thought.

Not so: today, on my computer map,
the line from our old house
to the Pal is an absolute straight shot.
It took twenty years for us
to name our malady:

we are *cartographically challenged.*

Maps are lost on us—more especially,
we are lost on maps. Given a compass,
we are all the more lost. We knew full well
that all the cowboys—Hopalong Cassidy
and our other heroes—lived full-time at the Pal.

More's the pity we failed the merit badge in maps.

On those Saturdays when, by serendipity,
we happened upon the Pal, we approached it
warily, like a desert mirage or religious shrine,
incredulous, yet full of faith. After all, when
the movie was over, we remained in danger—

of losing our selves on the way back home.

It's clear now that we were born
missing a link, minus something
like that inborn bit of iron that informs
all homing pigeons in one genetic swoop.

Nor did our malady improve with time:

Decades later, my grown-up brother,
babysitting two kids at a country funeral,
entertained them by tooling his car
along the gravel roads of the deep Piney Woods.

First, he reassured his passengers:

"Listen, guys. I don't want you to worry at all.
I know these back roads
like the palm of my hand." Minutes later,
he stopped the car, rolled the window down,
and yodeled,

"Hel-l-l-p!"

So it came to be that,
together with Christopher Columbus
we learned the value of being lost.
Which is how poetry entered the picture.

Poets, as it happens, are better off lost.

If they watch the world map
too closely, they may know more of
where to go, but less about what to say
when they arrive.

Like the voyages of Columbus,

poetry consists less of finding
what you set out to find, than in learning to live
with what you've stumbled across.

Most of this was rendered moot in 1948,

when I turned twelve:
I did a mighty pratfall across the intersection
of First Puberty Avenue and Main Street.

Simple times were about to get complex.

Some of the girls at my Junior High
seemed to know already, by heart,
the way to town and back.

I later figured out, on my own,

that in the years to come
if I found the right girl
she just might help me find the Pal.

And that turned out to be

deliciously true.

South Sycamore: The Horse

Jimmie Jack, a girl for sure,
lived right next door
and had an uncle

and he had a horse, for sure,
and he would bring it by her house
and let us ride.

And so we learned:
Always mount the horse
from the left side

Don't pull too hard
on the reins, boy
Easy does it better

Also don't kick the flanks.
The muzzle is made
to nuzzle—and the white star

for sure just like that on Trigger
the horse that Roy Rogers
reared and rared up on

at the Pal Theater
as the credits rolled
on Saturday afternoons

and he showed us how
it's supposed to be done
forever.

So Jimmie Jack rode,
then Uncle, then I.
Then Marler, my brother

for sure
climbed up
I would have guessed

even higher than Roy Rogers
and Trigger rared up
and Marler exited down—

well, he was dumped
unceremoniously, for sure
as though through

bomb bay doors
and hit the ground
as hard as China

Then with all the mysterious grace
that is child's play, he got back up,
ruefully, helping his pride

up, too, and grinning
And feeling in his back pocket
found a thin white handkerchief

and said to the amazed
bunch of us
A good thing I had this handkerchief

in my back pocket
I could have been
seriously hurt!

Halloween Impromptu

When the pumpkin's on the withered vine
in late October, next millennium,
I'll toast the pair of us again with wine
and trust that your dear ghost will come
to frighten mine.

Imagine with Me Now the Final Room

in memory of
Byron Herbert Reece
(1917–1958)

Imagine with me now the final room:
It need have no furniture—
just one chair

It need have no furniture
but pain.
And the gun, of course

not in full view, as if for show
but simply near the chair
Yes, that will do nicely, yes, *there.*

Just the chair and the pain
and the music:
Mozart.

And Wanda Landowska
whose fingers will know
what to do

Imagine with me now the final room
the man there now
and the chair and the pain

and the music
and the gun
and the fingers

that will know
exactly what to do.
And they do.

The Tuileries

From The *Louvre*, we hiked to *Place de la Concorde*
where, two hundred years ago, heads were lopped
and rolled, grimacing. Beyond the grilled gates we
stumbled on the bustling *Gardens*. The sun reflected

blindingly up from the white gravel. In that desert, we
spun with the carousel, clung madly to The Boomerang,
ate *frites et saucisses* with Coca-Cola Light
then rambled down the midway for ice cream.

It was then I felt the slightest nudge at my back.
Reaching for my shoulder pack, I found it
halfway open to the world. I spun around to look
for the enemy: they picked me out first

with their six blinkless eyes—a human tableau frozen
in the August heat: a dusty-faced mother and two sons,
maybe 8 and 12 years old. I might have called them gypsies
without knowing what I meant. I expected them to run,

so they didn't. They were still as garden statues,
as if they'd found their postures playing crack-the-whip,
the children's game in which no penalty came
unless they moved. They stared like deer transfixed

by the headlights of my eyes. They didn't move,
as though they could hear, in the distance, the prison doors
slam behind them; dead-still as thieves at punishment
about to lose not only the cunning of the hand,

but the hand itself. I clutched my bag and rifled
it myself: my wallet, camera, my passport, all there.
I knew then what was supposed to have happened next:
with my pack partway open, a business-like jostle

of my shoulder, a tourist, an easy mark, the jostle
and the smallest hand among them would have found
its way into the secret darkness of my pack.
I thought, only briefly, to grab my camera

and snap their cowering photograph.
But no gendarme was anywhere about. Besides,
I was afraid of the knife they surely had, hidden
among their flowing garments. In that moment

they sensed I'd given up. By imperceptible
degrees they began to move away from me
back into the crowd, as though re-entering
the history of this place from which they'd come,

this place that was always theirs—as though
they were stepping back into a pointillist painting,
a rendering of these gardens by Seurat, let's say,
the painting that includes now

this grove of trees by the garish midway
from which they had emerged
to confront me, their faces now taking on
the shapes of leaves, losing their details

in the green and human foliage,
until they are once again back in their element
beyond pain or terror or crime or execution
their sentence only that they may not leave these gardens

their passports valid forever
still poor
still hungry
still waiting

for the Revolution

· The Smell of Matches ·

(1972)

Cadaver

Fitting the labels
in our books
to our own tense tendons
slipping in their sheaths

we memorized the body
and the word

stripped the toughened skin
from the stringing nerve
the giving muscle.

Ribs sprang like gates.

In the chest
like archaeologists
we found it:
clotted, swollen,
aneurysmal
sign of an old sin—

the silent lust
that had buried itself
in the years

growing
in the hollow of his chest

still rounded by her arms
clinging
belly to belly
years beyond that first seed

to the rigid final fact

of a body.

To a Fourteen-Year-Old Girl
in Labor and Delivery

I cannot say it to you, Mother, Child.
Nowhere now is there a trace of the guile
that brought you here. Near the end of exile

I hold you prisoner, jailer, in my cage—
with no easy remedy for your rage
against him and the child. Your coming of age

is a time of first things: a slipping of latches;
of parallels like fire and the smell of matches.
The salmon swims upstream. The egg hatches.

Love Poem for a Son

I begin with you,
not red and wailing,
but small and round
in the upper tube,
where X met Y and multiplied,
in the soft cave of the uterus
where you caught and hung;
when notochord was spinal cord
and gut was gut forever;
when eyes were large,
as they still are;
and the heart was gathering
blood like flowers;
and what you started with
had to do.

You curled and uncurled
before the first breath
of anything but fluid,
and the thump of the mother
heart gave motion and all magic,
till you moved out like a little boat,
and came to me, red and weeping,
as even now you sometimes do.
I end with you.

A Thirty-Four-Year-Old Substitutes as Goalie
in Little League Soccer Practice

They are running
but I am out of breath.
My tie blows like a pennant,
green and yellow striped reminder
of what I must be tomorrow.

But now I am goalie.
The English in my blood
kicks at my ribs
watching the play.
My son, seven, at the end
of the field, runs
on his shin guards as though
he were born to them.

And they are coming my way,
miniature stallions,
snorting, faces contorting
toward the goal.

Boot it! Boot It!

and the boy boots it
with the energy of all
his eight years,
like a cannon ball,
but into my hands

and I have it,
I have it.

My toe dents the ball
to yells of victory.

And I trot to the sidelines
to huddle tall with my teammates
and my son,
sweaty, tired, proud as a bruise.

Talking to the Family

My white coat waits in the corner
like a father.
I will wear it to meet the sister
in her white shoes and organza dress
in the live of winter,

the milkless husband
holding the baby.

I will tell them.

They will put it together
and take it apart.
Their voices will buzz.
The cut ends of their nerves
will curl.

I will take off the coat,
drive home,
and replace the light bulb in the hall.

Autopsy in the Form of an Elegy

In the chest
in the heart
was the vessel

was the pulse
was the art
was the love

was the clot
small and slow
and the scar
that could not know

the rest of you
was very nearly perfect.

Lines on a Misread Word

> *. . . "bones and muscles" in his science book*
> *having been misread as "bones and musicals"*
> *by my seven-year-old son.*

My own bones are tired of talk;
they make no music when I walk,
but our skeletons together
have brought us nearer song than either
could have come to on his own.

And he will sing yet—not alone,
but, with some lighter female struts,
he'll dance in the air above these streets:
the two of them loop in the sun like kites
and not come down for days or nights

but sway like notes from xylophones
that play inside their musical bones.

The Bottle

Summers ago, after the woman
had moaned and birthed it
onto little more
than a kitchen table,

he sealed it in a bottle
while the sun bore down
and the patients waited.

In that long bath
it remains a monster
that couldn't live in air
but lasts in formalin

its forehead pressed against
the glass as though
against an endless window.

What magic did he use it for?
What lesson did it teach him

or his patient,
frightened anyway of what
the doctor might have to say
over his glasses

and the fetus
twenty years old on the shelf
staring at them both

believable as any genie.

Getting to Sleep in New Jersey

Not twenty miles from where I work,
William Williams wrote after dark,

after the last baby was caught,
knowing that what he really ought

to do was sleep. Rutherford slept,
while all night William Williams kept

scratching at his prescription pad,
dissecting the good lines from the bad.

He tested the general question whether
feet or butt or head-first ever

determines as well the length of labor
of a poem. His work is over:

bones and guts and red wheelbarrows;
the loneliness and all the errors

a heart can make the other end
of a stethoscope. Outside, the wind

corners the house with a long crow.
Silently, his contagious snow

covers the banks of the Passaic River,
where he walked once, full of fever,

tracking his solitary way
back to his office and the white day,

a peculiar kind of bright-eyed bird,
hungry for morning and the perfect word.

Being There

A doctor yourself,
    and you, a doctor's wife—
I like to believe
all you would have needed

was a kitchen table,
an aerosol of carbolic acid
against the bacteria seeding
from the cellar,
towels and water,

a teething ring
(from the first child)
for you to bite together.

Still I wanted you to know
how with a sweat, a smile,
an anxious cough,
my arms around you both,
I delivered your baby
from a long way off.

for Sandy and Jay Smith

Song for Tossing a Son

Bag of flour, sack of sand,
I toss you up and watch you lean
in air twice distant as my hand,
and higher than my head has seen.

The cry you make is one part terror;
the other half is laughing boy.
You fly with all my human error;
I bring you down with careful joy.

When you are older, wise and sure,
may you regain this oval track
that lets you rise in thinner air
till love and gravity pull you back.

da capo

So many mornings

in the long fraternity
of the house,
my cheeks puffed with sleep

till you,
your face rough with lather,

woke me conducting Brahms
and Bach by record

with your razor.

Rehearsal took ten years.

When I saw you last
you conducted an orchestra
we would have dreamed of
had we known enough.

Stravinsky stirred and laughed.
Mozart was still unburied.

Afterward
sprawling in a chair
you told me again
about music.

Grace notes poured
out of you like sweat.

for Samuel Jones

Coming Home

About two thousand miles
into my life
the family bounced south
west   east
in an old Oldsmobile.

Two brothers tumbled
on the back seat
watching the world blur
upside down right side up
through windows
time fogged in
slowly from the corners.

Nights
cars came at us
wall-eyed
their lights sliding
over the ceiling
like night fighters

while in the front
they talked parental   low
in a drone
we didn't hear
tossing through Arkansas
toward Mississippi.

When our eyes grew red
and blood bulged
in our heads from laughing
we slept

he on the seat
and I bent over
the humped transmission

close to the only motor
in the world.

· In All This Rain ·

(1980)

He Makes a House Call

Six, seven years ago
when you began to begin to faint
I painted your leg with iodine

threaded the artery
with the needle and then the tube
pumped your heart with dye enough

to see the valve
almost closed with stone.
We were both under pressure.

Today, in your garden,
kneeling under the sticky fig tree
for tomatoes

I keep remembering your blood.
Seven, it was. I was just
beginning to learn the heart

inside out.
Afterward, your surgery
and the precise valve of steel

and plastic that still pops and clicks
inside like a ping-pong ball.
I should try

chewing tobacco sometimes
if only to see how it tastes.
There is a trace of it at the corner

of your leathery smile
which insists that I see inside
the house: someone named Bill I'm supposed

to know; the royal plastic soldier
whose body fills with whiskey
and marches on a music box

How Dry I Am;
the illuminated 3-D Christ who turns
into Mary from different angles;

the watery basement,
the pills you take, the ivy
that may grow around the ceiling

if it must. Here, you
are in charge—of figs, beans,
tomatoes, life.

At the hospital, a thousand times
I have heard your heart valve open, close.
I know how clumsy it is.

But health is whatever works
and for as long. I keep thinking
of seven years without a faint

on my way to the car
loaded with vegetables
I keep thinking of seven years ago

when you bled in my hands like a saint.

Love Poem at a Particular Breakfast
for No Particular Woman

This blueberry muffin
is on its way to becoming
your breast.
It is only part-way there,
not nearly far enough,
smaller, harder.

Nothing is perfect.
It is better so. Of course.

But it makes me want
to taste you.

I'd like, some muffin-morning,
to love you like the last movement
of Mozart's 22nd Piano Concerto.

But this blueberry muffin
at breakfast
is as good a place as any
to begin.

Losing a Voice in Summer

How many parts rumble it was
how much gravel
dark, light
I don't remember

and it won't echo for me
from the shower stall

though sometimes off the porch
calling my own sons for supper
I can almost

almost hear it

as if you had let it go
out of the corner
of your mouth
like a ventriloquist
without a dummy.

I have no recording

otherwise I would play you
in the shower, repeat you
off the porch

from the cat-walk
of the glass factory have you sing
Go Down Moses
over and over and

tonight
with the reluctant sentence
deep in my head at the hoarsest hour,
dumb and laryngitic and alone

I first understood
how completely I have lost your voice,
father, along with my own.

Love Poem Entirely of Clichés

Breathing a word
but strictly between us

there is this about you

on the one hand
or the other

on the tip of my tongue.

You of all things
and of all people.

A Cliché Poem for Your Leaving

Last things first.
I would not by the hair of my chin
utter a word against you
except to ask where in hell
is the silver lining.

No news is not necessarily

says the philosopher, pleased
with himself, his head buried,
and as always, just enough off
the mark of the real world
to appear as wise as he is old.

I hope to God

I don't pass this way again.
As it is the best place to end
was at the beginning
as it were.
For the time being

holding the short end of the stick

I mean to contemplate
only until six of one
seems once more
half a dozen.
I am well, also alive.

It's just a matter of time
until the truth
will out.
Till then, I am resigned
in name only and, as before
left to my own devices.

Death

I have seen   come on
slowly as rust
sand

or suddenly   as when
someone leaving
a room

finds the doorknob
come loose in his hand

Double-Header

Each and every one of us has got a schedule to keep.
—A TRUCK DRIVER BEING INTERVIEWED ON RADIO

I've made it
have been left alone in the stadium
locked here after the baseball
twilight game, having hidden
where I won't tell

on a bet with someone I invented
and therefore had to win.
I can hear the Security Guard
locking up, watch him making his way out,
turning off the lights as he goes

toward home and supper, away from
the smell of popcorn and beer.
I can see him look
with a question at my car,
the only one besides his

still in the lot and see him
look back once at the stadium without
knowing or even thinking I could be
looking back at him, my face barbed
with wire. I turn now to the stadium

that is all mine, bought
with my money, purchased with
a three-dollar ticket for the top tier,
the stadium that is coming alive again
with the crowd that is coming back

but of course isn't coming back
to watch me play, with DiMaggio in center,
Cobb in left, Hornsby at second
Rizzuto at short, and all the others
who have been tagged out more than once

themselves, and who will get me later
or sooner, trying to stretch a single
into a double, catching up with my lost breath
that I can remember now from when
I was eleven, with a stitch in my side

sprinting still in spite of the stitch
for the inside-the-park home run
I almost had when I was twelve
for the girl I almost got when I got
old enough but didn't know the rules

dusting my pants off now
to the music I never learned, for
the symphony orchestra I never conducted,
my hands rough with rosin
for the truck I never drove

and the fish I never caught
and wouldn't have known if I had
how to take him off the hook,
for my father who is in the crowd
cheering out his heart

but who of course isn't there
as I pull up lame at second
with a stand-up double
in this game that goes on for hours,
my hands stinging with the bat,

the All-Stars aligned against me
in this stadium I own for the night,
one great circle and inside this circle
this square that seems the only one
on this curving darkening ball of earth

or the only one anyway
marked by bases I must run all night
for everything I should
by now
be worth.

The Girl in the Hall

with the Mickey Mouse
watch tells me the time

without knowing

that I have come up
the stairs
from a crushed leg
scared eyes

and the stump
blood   bandages

the bones of the stretcher

he is gradually getting used to

the fact of no leg
below the knee
no toes to wiggle
though they move still
in his mind's foot

which remembers now only
the crane coming down on it.

She glances at her wrist.

In his head's watch
in the middle of morphine
he clutches the giant hands
like Harold Lloyd holding on
at half past five
while the cars line up
below him.

The expressway roars outside.

She asks.
I say I'm fine.

She has her clocks.
He, his.
I, mine.

Helping with the Math Homework

In the beginning
there were polynomials

differences of squares
trial and error

and the sum of two cubes.
X^2 minus Y^2

has always had
the same meaning

whatever it is.
But when Pythagoras

looked into
the eye of the triangle

and saw the solution
I wasn't there.

Nor have I ever found
anything more

than safety in numbers.
This is the new math

these are your problems
and I was born

before the back of the book.
What I have been saying is this:

I can lead you
only so far into wisdom.

Soon
you must begin to learn

how to be ignorant
on your own.

Lessons in the Subjunctive

That the door be opened
    the knob whispers
    to the hinges

That the child be found
    the grass is bent
    in the direction
    of his sleeping

That the midnight come
    the clock admits
    its only habit

That there be some kind of answer
    the tongue lies in its teeth

That the war be over
    the war is over

That the violin play
    the fingers leap and glide

That the string may say

That the bow decide

One Evening

And he said *for God's sake*
looking Death in the kisser

they said *how much insulin*
water
how much digitalis

and he said *I need a drink*
and he didn't mean water

they said *the rules don't*
allow it
about the time

Hutchins was catching
the long pass on the three

yard line and tripping
forward for the touchdown
about the time

the father was saying
go to sleep and I don't mean

maybe half the world
was standing on their heads
and didn't give an

anyway the sun came up
the time was recorded and copies

made about the time
all 14 billion milliequivalents
of him said in a loud barely but

audible voice
to hell with this

Bringing Her Home

While you were in the hospital
the house was sick as hell.

I should have said the children
are well. And the turtles.

The kettle was cured with singing.

But your dresses
were breathless in the closet.
And then the demented washer
began to knock while spinning;
the dryer died wet as diapers.
And in one seizure of wind
the hinges on the doors
got palsy.

All last night
I was afraid of mushrooms.

No matter now.
The children and the turtles
are waiting for you there.
They are well.

But the close-mouthed keyholes and I
have been gasping for air.

Looking Down into a Ditch

Watching the workmen dig a ditch
watching them lay in the pipe

for the waste and gasses
and liquids of our living

I think of the lost maps
of lost cities, their pipes
still moving off
in important directions

of people I knew
who are now in the serious dirt

of the ditches at Dachau

of my father.

It is hard
to keep remembering
across the ditches we have made
and covered over
with terrible earth-moving sound

how much of our dying
we must find ways not to need,
how much of what keeps us alive
is underground.

How I'd Have It

I'd have no flowers
other than Mozart

A suit—blue—
not new, but worn

the knees
still in the trousers

for as long
as polyester is

And a fire
and someone there

to throw on
the oak especially

for the last movement
of the Mozart

As for the mourners
let's have them enter

STAGE LEFT
and pause and peer

over the side
and say mournful

things such as What
A Pity A Pity

And So Old, Too.
And then exit all

STAGE RIGHT

Building the Steps

She said to me
after I had already started
at the top

always start at the bottom
and I believed her
but as I say

I had already started
and at that
at the top

She had that look
on her face
one has to believe

She will be
when I finish
surely at the bottom

As I place the last stone
she must be first
to try them out

Up they must go and down
equally well
for either of us

like the road to town
like the bones of my back
hoping the last step

is where her foot
would have it
up as she wants it now

or down

Whittling: The Last Class

What has been written
about whittling
is not true

most of it

It is the discovery
that keeps
the fingers moving

not idleness

but the knife looking for
the right plane
that will let the secret out

Whittling is no pastime

he says
who has been whittling
in spare minutes at the wood

of his life for forty years

Three rules he thinks
have helped
Make small cuts

In this way

you may be able to stop before
what was to be an arm
has to be something else

Always whittle away from yourself

and toward something.
For God's sake
and your own

know when to stop

Whittling is the best example
I know of what most
may happen when

least expected

bad or good
Hurry before
angina comes like a pair of pliers

over your left shoulder

There is plenty of wood
for everyone
and you

Go ahead now

May you find
in the waiting wood
rough   unspoken

what is true

or
nearly true
or

true enough.

The Truck

I was coming back from
wherever I'd been when
I saw the truck and
the sign on the back repeated
on the side to be certain
you knew it was no mistake

PROGRESS CASKETS

ARTHUR ILLINOIS

Now folks have different
thoughts it's true about
death but in general it's
not like any race for
example you ever ran
everyone wanting to come in

last and all   And I admit
a business has to have a good
name   No one knows better
than I the value of a good
name   A name is what sells
the product in the first

and in the final place
All this time the Interstate
was leading me into Atlanta
and I was following the sign
and the truck was heavier
climbing the hill than

going down which is as
it should be   What I really
wanted to see was the driver
up close maybe talk to him
find out his usual run
so I could keep off it

Not that I'm superstitious   It's just
the way I was raised   A casket
may be Progress up in Arthur
but it's thought of
down here
as a setback.

Answering the Phone

Used to
you'd say
Hello
and think nothing of it

or someone else might do it
for you
He's out may I take a message
and you'd return the call

When Bobby died
and the man across the street
and Bill
and Mr. G.

all that changed
and you think
now before you answer the phone
you take a deep breath

and think something of it
and you know
no one else can ever answer
for you again

so now you pick up the receiver
and say not hello but
now what

now what

Fugue

*. . . the most highly developed
form of contrapuntal imitation
based on the principle of the
equality of the parts.*

This, dear, is *presto*
   and this *sostenuto*
Now for *glissando*
   a sliding of winds

A slight *ritardando*
   is all I can manage
such *appassionato*
   the music portends

We've tried it *con brio*
   bolero, calmato
a tempo, crescendo
   (The curtain descends)

You are the *alto*
   to my *basso buffo*
The score says *legato*
   The tempo depends

on the mood of the maestro
   And now *furioso*
con moto, sforzando!
   With what *accordando*

this symphony ends.

In All This Rain

for Doktor Bruder,
the dachshund

Despite
what is written
about the rain

love is the one element
that takes more sense
than any other

to know when
to come in out of.
It rains

sooner or later of course on
everything we bury
And burying a dog

is not
according to the experts
supposed to be anything like

as painful
as burying your kin.
They say

think of it as a sleep
in which the stars also
all go out at once

the stars that you know
are still up there
but just can't see.

I stopped
a long time ago trying
to make sense

out of all this business
of giving up the ghost.
I find no consolation

in this brown fact
of your dying
which reminds me only

that no man
is any deader
than his dog.

I don't believe
you're better off.
Those of us looking up

can still see the stars
at least when it's
not raining. We've kept

the box
of a house where you lived
49 years of a dog's life.

I'd like you to know
that when I told Jim,
"Dok's gone,"

he said,
"You mean he's dead."
And went over to the couch

where you used to sprawl.
And cried.
Later he said,

"Next dog
I want one that lasts."

· Renaming the Streets ·

(1985)

Early Sunday Morning

Edward Hopper, 1930

Somewhere in the next block
someone may be practicing the flute
but not here

where the entrances
to four stores are dark
the awnings rolled in

nothing open for business
Across the second story
ten faceless windows

In the foreground
a barber pole, a fire hydrant
as if there could ever again

be hair to cut
fire to burn
And far off, still low

in the imagined East
the sun that is again
right on time

adding to the Chinese red
of the building
despite which color

I do not believe
the day
is going to be hot

It was I think
on just such a day
it is on just such a morning

that every Edward Hopper
finishes, puts down his brush
as if to say

As important
as what is
happening

is what is not.

Rosemary

Little Rock, Arkansas
October 26, 1982

6 A.M. All over the world
people are sleeping in shifts.
Rosemary is my waitress.

Not only is she beautiful
she brings me food and herbs
from the stores of her pantry.

From the looks of her
the legs are the last to go.
To, fro, she has a most remarkable walk

anatomy-proud, pendulum-perfect.
Does she have children
a husband   asleep

off somewhere in this remote new day?
It's ill-advised to ask such questions
yet they're what I'd like to know

after an evening
in the arms of the Sheraton.
Last names are never put

on name tags now
have you noticed?
They could be used as proof.

Besides
a last name is too intimate.
A name tag like *Rosemary*

is properly civil
opaque as a servant.
I tell her my name is John.

There is a buffet
which I approach under the gaze
of a Jack O'Lantern

set up against those
who would take too much bacon.
I choose freely, with the magical joy

of hunger, taking some extra bacon
and stroll back with my plate.
There is so much

I'd like to have Rosemary tell me
but she pirouettes
constantly, table to table

pouring coffee,
resetting the places
for the other nameless

numb nightcrawlers
descended from
their Posturized beds

into the subdued light
of this morning place.
The businessmen

are reading the grim papers,
wiping their mouths, leaving,
a gnaw now in their upper abdomens.

My fourth cup of coffee
is strong, doing
its intravenous work.

Suddenly I realize that Rosemary and I
are alone in this place.
She sits herself down

at a table across the room
to have her own quick breakfast.
The sun is coming in through her hair.

I want to call her over, say
Rosemary, sit down
then read her this poem.

But there is no such thing
as a simple pleasure.
I have the feeling she knows

it is already too late for poems.
All over Little Rock
in great Brownian motion

all of the others
are waking up
just as we feared they would.

January: A Flight of Birds

Watching the birds, I think of Bach,
each of the distant wheeling flock

a black note on a turning page,
the darkened afternoon the stage.

Watching their wide, then narrow belt
I imagine how Bach felt,

with hundreds of melodies all at once,
inventing his own celestial stunts.

In their equivalent of cantata
the birds perform a short fermata

then in silent sky-bound bugle
swoop and go, their music fugal.

I think of their flight in terms of Master
Bach at his keyboard, writing vaster

harmonies than the court could dream—
which is why, in pure esteem,

the world would be, if Bach- and bird-less,
as much diminished as if wordless.

Forecast

I can wade Grief—
Whole Pools of it
—EMILY DICKINSON

It started raining Grief tonight
in purest barometric blunder—
hard Grief, merciless, despite

the forecast—which made me wonder
why we of all had to be chosen—
but since Grief fell from such a height

and since the darkness now is frozen,
that Grief is turning into snow,
crunching underneath our feet

quieting the traffic's flow
taking the shapes of our charades
until the sun compels its rise

as Grief and Light must always meet
and the temperature persuades
Grief's slow invisible demise.

She in February

is more
than the sum
of her parts

her breath
sleep   her walk
her lup

dup
not to mention
of course

her unmentionables
such
as

her brain waves
delta and alpha
which go on

and on
and which
like the smell

of her hair
have been carefully
recorded.

You Round the Bend

of the expressway
just at dusk
there is something in the road

as you hurtle toward it
all you know is
that you want it not to be

something that ever had
the possibility
of loving

because
whatever it is
it's dead

And it's unavoidably
under your wheels
It's a rolled-up carpet just

a carpet, old and worn
You drive on, taking in
and letting out a sigh because

you know that such a circumstance
can be complicated
and you are glad

this once that it isn't.

The Eclipse

Atlanta
May 30, 1984

The day of the eclipse began like any other.
I'd thought one god or another might call it off.
By eleven, though, the sun high, I guessed

they were planning to go on through with it.
Already, crowds of people with smoked glass,
armed with blankets, chairs, beer and wine

against the universe, were swarming their curious
ways to the open country of the park.
Only a limited amount of work can be done

on a day scheduled to be cut in half,
making two holidays where there were none. I went
along as disbeliever to watch what clearly

was out of my hands. There was nothing brusque
about what happened next. Only the sun
dependably overhead and hot—and then

the slow diminuendo wash of dusk:
a perceptible chill, a slight moon-lit wind,
all the gullible street lamps coming on,

the birds ruffling in uneasy slurs,
tree to tree. Then false dawn, in which
those trees relearned their shadows. And it was over.

A woman was heard to say *It didn't last
long enough. It never does,* I said.
But what we all remembered most was the drunk

who'd waited both days and most of his life to ask
those of us still lounging in the park,
as the real sun was relentlessly going down:

Is this the eclipse? Or is it just getting dark?

Three for the Mona Lisa

1

It is not what she did
at 10 o'clock
last evening

accounts for the smile

It is
that she plans
to do it again

tonight.

2

Only the mouth
all those years
ever

letting on.

3

It's not the mouth
exactly

it's not the eyes
exactly either

it's not even
exactly a smile

But, whatever,
I second the motion.

Gaudeamus Igitur: A Valediction

For this is the day of joy
      which has been fourteen hundred and sixty days in coming
For today in the breathing name of Brahms
      and the cat of Christopher Smart
      through the unbroken line of language and all the nouns
      stored in the angular gyrus
      today is a commencing
For this is the day you know too little
      against the day when you will know too much
For you will be invincible
      and vulnerable in the same breath
      which is the breath of your patients
For their breath is our breathing and our reason
For the patient will know the answer
      and you will ask him
      ask her
For the family may know the answer
For there may be no answer
      and you will know too little again
      or there *will* be an answer and you will know too much forever
For you will look smart and feel ignorant
      and the patient will not know which day it is for you
      and you will pretend to be smart out of ignorance
For you must fear ignorance more than cyanosis
For whole days will move in the direction of rain
For you will cry and there will be no one to talk to
      or no one but yourself
For you will be lonely
For you will be alone
For there is a difference
For there is no seriousness like joy
For there is no joy like seriousness
For the days will run together in gallops and the years
      go by as fast as the speed of thought
      which is faster than the speed of light
      or Superman
      or Superwoman
For you will not be Superman
For you will not be Superwoman

For you will not be Solomon[*]
     but you will be asked the question nevertheless
For after you learn what to do, how and when to do it
     the question will be *whether*
For there will be addictions: whiskey, tobacco, love
For they will be difficult to cure
For you yourself will pass the kidney stone of pain
     and be joyful
For this is the end of examinations
For this is the beginning of testing
For Death will give the final examination
     and everyone will pass
For the sun is always right on time
     and even that may be reason for a kind of joy
For there are all kinds of
     all degrees of joy
For love is the highest joy
For which reason the best hospital is a house of joy
     even with rooms of pain and loss
     exits of misunderstanding
For there is the mortar of faith
For it helps to believe
For Mozart can heal and no one knows where he is buried
For penicillin can heal
     and the word
     and the knife
For the placebo will work and you will think you know why
For the placebo will have side effects and you will know you do not
     know why
For none of these may heal
For joy is nothing if not mysterious
For your patients will test you for spleen
     and for the four humors
For they will know the answer
For they have the disease
For disease will peer up over the hedge
     of health, with only its eyes showing

---

[*] 1 Kings 3:16–27

For the T waves will be peaked and you will not know why
For there will be computers
For there will be hard data and they will be hard to understand
For the trivial will trap you and the important escape you
For the Committee will be unable to resolve the question
For there will be the arts
       and some will call them
       soft data
       whereas in fact they are the hard data
       by which our lives are lived
For everyone comes to the arts too late
For you can be trained to listen only for the oboe
       out of the whole orchestra
For you may need to strain to hear the voice of the patient
       in the thin reed of his crying
For you will learn to see most acutely out of
       the corner of your eye
       to hear best with your inner ear
For there are late signs and early signs
For the patient's story will come to you
       like hunger, like thirst
For you will know the answer
       like second nature, like first
For the patient will live
       and you will try to understand
For you will be amazed
       or the patient will not live
       and you will try to understand
For you will be baffled
For you will try to explain both, either, to the family
For there will be laying on of hands
       and the letting go
For love is what death would always intend if it had the choice
For the fever will drop, the bone remold itself along
       its lines of force
       the speech return
       the mind remember itself
For there will be days of joy
For there will be elevators of elation

and you will walk triumphantly
in purest joy
along the halls of the hospital
and say *Yes* to all the dark corners
where no one is listening
For the heart will lead
For the head will explain
but the final common pathway is the heart
whatever kingdom may come
For what matters finally is how the human spirit is spent
For this is the day of joy
For this is the morning to rejoice
For this is the beginning
Therefore, let us rejoice
Gaudeamus igitur.

The Pigeon Sonnets

for Ron and Keith Schuchard

HOMING PIGEON I

Its house as handsome as a Henry Moore
a prisoner in the rounded sleep of egg
being embryo could be a bore:
a rudimentary heart, a wing, a leg.

But then the chipping chisel of its beak—
a burglar on the perfect inside job—
and with a novice's display of cheek
what began as instinct ends as squab.

Three weeks later mother throws a curve
forcing the youngling from the yawning nest
to fall back onto sheer ancestral nerve
and the assumption that such is for the best.

  Whether feathered or in human skin
  in the beginning the trick is to begin.

Rising to risk a thousand miles away
wings whipping like a metronome
the bird circles and conjures up the way:
two days later he swoops back down—at home.

A feat of such Lindberghian *esprit*
must mystify the pigeons in the park.
It summons up no less than awe in me
pleased to find the bathroom in the dark.

Exactly how it's done remains the question:
By sleight-of-wing? By avian ESP?
I doubt that science, with intricate digestion,
will ever explicate this pedigree

   though all of us in time will have to steer
   the wordless distances from there to here.

Surely, one mile up, there is the lure
of flying past the loft, of foreign intrigue,
of what might yet be his, of one detour
before clear signs of structural fatigue;

maybe taking off some Saturday
to Rio or New York or even France,
reborn into the world as emigré
all future landings left strictly to chance.

Still, though some are lost to hawks or cats
and some go down in perfect cloudless weather
most do return, ending with pirouettes
above the loft, resummoned by some tether

like monks assembling, like most of us, reshaping
the wondrous burden of our not escaping.

Misdirected (I thought), a pigeon perched
at the windowsill tonight, a gray surprising
rustle in the open bay. He lurched,
bustled, and bobbed his head, as though surmising

lights meant love—and this might be the place
expecting the note (I imagine now) he carried.
Slow-witted, I tried to shoo him out of grace:
even-toed, composed, he would not be harried.

No, he tilted his head to investigate,
extending his neck to survey my room; conveying
less than a myna might of where you wait,
serene as a dove in the game (I've guessed) you're playing.

Oblique in love as a shy medieval pen,
necessary one, would you write—again?

The shortest way between two distances
is this quad. The bird, a baritone,
with all of Romeo's insistences,
banks pidgin-English off the ancient stone.

The lover gargles loudly, but to whom?
Amplified as through a microphone
to resonate more roundly in my room
the sum of all his sound is monotone.

I have no doubt that she will reappear:
Though it's the season to doubt everything,
that pigeons mate for life is also clear.

I move he wait her out, at least till spring:
A love is someone who can always hear
the only music you can ever sing.

A Word from the Teacher

In the first grade
for this unit
we are studying
The Age of the Dinosaurs
We are also making
an exhibit to be shown
at PTA

Everyone except Johnny
wanted to make
a Stegosaurus
or a Tyrannosaurus rex
out of clay

Johnny preferred to make
a Brontosaurus
which explains

why the demography
of our dinosaur population
may seem somewhat
out of kilter

Nevertheless
the whole class
has been involved
in this demonstration
and we are almost ready
to represent
several hundred millennia

using a backdrop of green
posterboard, the dinosaur
models, of course

and at least a hundred
small clay pellets
meant to be eggs
and not whatever
petrified else
you may have been thinking
they were

By working together
we have learned much
in the preparation
of this interesting exhibit

which may yet win
First Prize
and make our inscrutable parents
proud at last

We thought of having
special music
to go with our
display
but we couldn't agree
as a class

on just what kind of music
dinosaurs
might have preferred

while on their way
to what everyone knows
came next:

a big fat zero

To tell you the truth
the whole thing
leaves me
a little sad

the way
every day
always
somewhere
sometime
someone

is having to start all over

November

1. Early

The earliest leaves are now
starting to fall. Those
that did contrive somehow

in autumn's swift revision
to cling a moment more
have turned in pure precision

burned yellow, brown,
red, ochre, gold
in every part of town

as though replying to
a question I never heard.
If color is a clue

I take all this to mean
whatever the answer was
it couldn't be said in green.

2. Late

"Hope" is the thing with feathers
—EMILY DICKINSON

Out in the weather
the waterproof birds
hoping together
exempted from words

this is my time
the fall of the leaf
that imperfect crime
finale of grief

summer's illusion
a figure of speech
August's intrusion
cast off on the beach

December ahead
white as the distance
frost overspread
at winter's insistence

the chances of spring
little more than a guess
whatever the question
the answer is *yes.*

December

At the bottom of the hill
on which stands
one of the grandest houses

in town
past which I drive daily
on my way to tend

the sickest poor
in town
a woman in a blue

silk dressing gown
just before Christmas
is vigorously poking

a long stick
down into two huge rolling
garbage cans

which she has just brought out
to the curb
from the house

poking the stick down
hard so that the tops
will fit the cans

so that some degree
of equanimity
may attend the day.

By such incongruities
is the free world
saved.

The Bass

Because I was 37 and he was 10
I was presumed and of course
to know everything important

plus
how to take the fish off the hook.
I'd been told largemouth

and striped bass
both   either
waited for us below

the still crystal of the lake
I had no expectation though
of actually catching a fish

when somehow we did
After we hauled it heavily
in over the gunwales

like a glittering glory
no way was I about to touch
that wide mouth, those razor fins

gills, those sparkling cold-blooded
scales
until all spasm stopped

To this day my son
may think the way
to take a fish off the hook

is to place it, hook still intact
in the bottom of the boat
place a paddle over the fish

and keep your foot gently but steadfastly
on the paddle on the fish
After the flailing and flopping

I managed with something like
experience to get the hook out
Then as morning broke over us

we made our slow electric way
back to the boathouse
That fish won for us

a trophy
which I keep here on my desk
to remind me of that morning and of

how unexpected the end may be
how hungry
how shining

· Where Water Begins ·

(1998)

Where Water Begins

Butler Mountain
Cherry Log, Georgia

Because it was July all over town
because they had a cabin in the mountains
whence cometh our help, we took off Friday

afternoon and headed for the hills:
he, his wife, and I: two Jacks and Jill.
Within two hours, we gunned the car up steeply

shooting the gravel down the road behind us
and landed on a small, bulldozed plateau.
Down below, the cabin in the trees

and more than a hundred straight down feet, the creek
making its changing sense on down the mountain.
I breathed in deeply three thousand feet of air

threw down my bag and fishing gear and sprawled
and listened to the water in its wonder.
Tom and Nancy set about to see

that all was in its place, which it was.
Tom got down on hands and knees to turn
the faucet handle underground to let

the water flow into the house, not from
the creek, but deeper, pumped uphill
from a well we all believed was there.

The faucet's only answer was rushing air.
He and I slid down the hill to find
the pump's problem: a broken water pipe

it wouldn't take a plumber to diagnose
but clearly would to make the water flow.
As we trudged back up, I thought of Auden

which could be a first for this mountain:
"Thousands have lived without love, not one
without water." Only the cactus and the desert rat

I thought, recalling my physiology.
At least the lights were on, glory be
for electrons in the wires. Hot dogs

were ready: and in the purring refrigerator
three cold beers, a couple of jugs of wine.
We ate, I drank the beer, thanking the stars

Tom and Nancy never liked the stuff.
After supper they walked to the nearest phone
to call for help: no answer. The only way

to stay here was to haul from the creek
backbreaking water up in buckets
to prime the toilets, and to borrow drinking

water in plastic bottles from the neighbor's
bountiful tap: no bath, no shower, only
a light brushing of the teeth, then sleep.

When the sun broke through the window of
my room next morning, I heard the resourceful two
making breakfast for us in the kitchen.

I pulled on clean socks and last night's jeans
and joined them on the deck above the creek
which burbled and taunted us from down below.

This was the day for fishing, so we did:
caught eight bream and threw all back but two.
Balanced carefully lest the canoe tip over—

we almost even made it back to shore.
Water is one thing, mud another.
We sponged off at a fountain by the church.

By now the missing maintenance man was home.
But it was late Saturday afternoon
and Tom had heard his promises before.

We cooked out on the grill—steaks, corn,
the two bream our fishing trip had fooled.
And listened to Mozart, Schubert, Mahler.

And slept with water running in our heads.
But not inside the cabin. Next morning
the taps as dry as stone, as diabetes,

we shrugged: what's one more day of pheromones?
Sunday. We ate and read and dozed and walked.
At dusk, as we loaded up the car

it was Nancy's unexpecting hand
that turned the kitchen tap and, by God
and gravity, there was water in

the pipes: too late, but there it was, choking
on the air within the main, battling
against itself and swallowing mercifully—

the grace of water, water everywhere.
And so we ended in a kind of dance
in praise of gods or goddesses unknown

who bid the water run. We opened all
the taps, flushed and smiled and watched the toilets'
counterclockwise perfect swirling, welcomed

the obedient sputtering uphill flow.
And drank. And one last time we opened
up the line and listened for the gurgle

and the cough. Then cut the water off.

    for Tom and Nancy Sellers

Poem on an Accidental Xerox of Her Hand

for Delese Wear

Dermatoglyphics is the fancy name
for the gentle science of reading palms

or, for that matter, soles: anywhere
genetics takes its chances and leaves lines.

Fortune-tellers make whole lives of such
cutaneous meanderings, of course,

taking the intersections of the world
as each presents itself, heart in hand.

I could have used some palmistry today:
A woman in Ohio, sending poems,

xeroxed not only the poet's finest frenzy,
but also, at the upper left, her hand.

That is the wondrous way the world may happen—
you start to do one thing and do another.

Up to now I haven't read the poem.
I've only sat here hoping to say sooth,

trying to glean a message from this map,
life line, love line, shape of her own sweet time.

La Ci Darem La Mano[*] hums through my head.
For having seen their tracery in the air,

five slender ministers practicing their Braille,
I swear by the metacarpal hills of fortune

I would have known these fingers anywhere.

---

[*]There we will take each other by the hand

124

October

There was the late light
and the bird breaking
its wings against the air

and the light diminishing

and the bird seeking
shelter
for at least the night

and the bird diminishing.

Love is not too strong a word for it.

Next Door

of a sudden
with no fanfare
but much finesse

the gingko that
has blazed all month
has acquiesced

in a swirl of fans

and now stands
in a pool of yellow
like a woman

who has just slipped out
of her dress.
Will all those who agree

please raise their hands?

Holiday

Martin Luther King, Jr., Birthday, 1995

Early, early. I back the car
down the driveway.
The world is asleep.

It's rained all night
and the blackboard
of sky

on which the answers
by now
should have been written

is still clean and wordless.
In the restaurant
the air is noisy

with loud faces
that laugh and chatter
as though this were a morning

feast imagined by Brueghel.
I order an un-holiday
breakfast: grits with American

cheese, extra hot, buttered rye.
From the looks of the *New York Times*
there is still plenty of terror

to go around. Nevertheless, today
I am grateful. For words. For the occasional
evidences of love. For strong coffee.

On the way home, little traffic.
I nudge the Camry up the driveway. The garage
door rumbles down faithfully behind me.

I put on some Bach.
There may be time this morning
to write a poem

if one will venture in
out of the weather.
Outside, it's rained all night.

The world is cool
and washed and, other days,
would be almost ready for school.

But, of course,
today there is no school.
And even if there were

there is no teacher.

The Good-bye, Good-Morning, Hello Poem

Halloween 1984, Chicago

By the unluck of the draw
bypassed by the Palmer House,
the Hyatt, the Marriott

I am nonetheless sheltered
in Chicago: put up
in a blue and pink motel

called Traveler's Rest,
its logo a mystified flamingo.
I am housed on the third floor

above the single-minded traffic
in a room out of Hopper.
I turn the key—the door squeaks

like no casket should.
Flipping the switch
inside the room

flicks on the yellow bedside lamp
but also startles the TV set
into full commercial roar.

The room is warm
the temperature control knob
on the wall falls loose in my hand.

The shower
has a single setting: *Bruise.*
And the perfect touch:

One wall of this room
has a sliding glass patio door
with—my God—no patio outside.

No anything outside but air
and three long stories down
the parking lot.

I have prayed three nights here
not to sleepwalk in Chicago
so as not to conclude like the coyote

in those roadrunner cartoons
who zips straight off the precipice
hesitates, double-takes

then plummets.
The mattress slopes relentlessly
toward the patio that isn't there.

For hours I have slept uphill
as though pinned down at Iwo Jima
clutching all night

at the slippery gravel of sleep.
Finally the wake-up noise
of traffic brings me to

on the median of a highway
in my head.
I flip the switch

and bring the sleeping room to life
the TV on:
The announcer says first thing

Indira Gandhi is dead
shot by her military guard.
What new bad dream is this?

And after the brief commercial break
the newscaster reminds me
that Harry Houdini died on Halloween

his abdomen tight as a boil.
Despite the terrors of the world
I'm hungry. I rise, shower, am bruised.

I dress and stumble
across the manic streets
to take a seat at Chicken Supreme.

I order the special for two-ninety-nine
watch it cooked and served
by a whirling dervish

in his perfect element.
Awash with coffee
I stroll back to the rumpled room:

The message light is blinking. *Now what?*
I lift the receiver and listen—
a friend's unexpected voice:

"John Keats was born today in 1795."
Oh, bless you, friend.
And bless you, too

Little John
and bless us all
under the October sky.

In this bustling place
we are forever
lifting a toast to one

and mourning another,
Halloween or not, every day.
I pay the motel bill.

My taxi comes.
Over his shoulder
the driver smiles

and says, "Good morning."
I ask him if it really
is a good morning.

He says, "Sure is, sure is:
a lotta guys won't be gettin' up at all
this morning—*got* to be good."

I lean back and puff my pipe
all the way to the airport
glad for the personal art that is a life

in awe of the bitter physics of the world
with nowhere to go but down
the prospects for love

as uncertain as tuberculosis.
Yes sir, I'm *glad* to be up
this morning.

Good-bye, Harry Houdini
Rest, Indira Gandhi,
Good-bye, Chicago blue and pink

Good-bye, motel, patio door,
magic, television,
and the national insanities.

Hello, love.

This Kind of Thing Doesn't Happen Often
and When It Does You Should Pay Attention

*i thank heaven somebody's crazy
enough to send me a daisy*
—E.E. CUMMINGS

On Piedmont Road, going north,
before my car there floated forth

a soapy bubble in the traffic,
glistening and holographic.

It drifted down into my path,
this ghostly sphere from someone's bath.

I watched it bob and almost tickle
a Harley-Davidson motorcycle

then rise (as it got quite exhausted).
That's where I left it, fair and frosted.

For this unexpected act
I thank heaven (I think), in fact,

that someone went to all the trouble
to blow me a bubble.

He Attends Exercise Class—Once

for Sally Wolff King

Incongruous as it feels, I lie stretched out,
making compromises with my bones,
gathered here with colleagues, mostly stout.
Though some of us will wheeze like saxophones,

the veterans contort and bend with ease,
even those weighed down with many stone.
I sweat and write, in vivid fantasies,
a book called Some Positions I Have Known.

And gradually the drill gets even harder:
a sergeant in a skimpy uniform
keeps time by counting, with Germanic ardor,
maneuvers calculated to deform.

Among the twenty prisoners are the dean,
a monster in a purple leotard,
and I, whose mind has labored to be lean,
whose body, up to now, has been unscarred.

The exercises are designed to rout
the oleaginous treachery of fat.
As we end, no one of us can doubt
the common denominator of the mat.

My serial number and my rank and name
are all they know about me, thinking back.
But the world can never be the same
to one who's known the terror of the rack.

After the Concert: A Confession

It was that string quintet by Brahms:
in F—the one that starts *allegro*
then in the second movement suddenly

turns *grave ed appassionato:* Remember?
That second movement was so full
of grace, viola singing so, the cello

grave and joyful both at once.
And there we were, you and I,
side by side by thigh breathing together.

So in the finale, in the glory
of that last fugue, *allegro energico*, it was,
when all heaven was breaking loose

I want you to know

now that the concert is over
and you have gone back
to your love and I to mine

I want you to know

how much, there in the middle of it all,
right there in front of God and everybody
how much I wanted to

ask you to dance.

5 A.M., SLEEPLESS IN MERTON STREET

I open the windows and let the morning in.
The music is Bach, unaccompanied violin.

The sun's up, the same unruly Sunne
unwelcomed by the languorous John Donne

flaccid after too much love or sex.
His pigeons' kin say *Yes* with all their necks

still not smart enough to say or show
when they mean *No.*

The sun comes early here and stays late.
Just after nine at night, the night must wait

as Christ Church summons with bells her hundred and one.
That ghostly roll call occupies the sun

while the college clocks bicker toward ten.
Even England is tired of sun by then

and glad to watch the last light ratchet down
all over town.

Atop this house, my two rooms make an aerie,
a teacher's nest, a writer's solitary.

The curtains whip in air both brisk and sunny.
I make the tea and sweeten the day with honey.

Here, messages abound: in the *sostenuto*
of Merton's bells, the Italian choir on radio.

The wind in the curtains tells the future and more,
but in semaphore.

The whole world's a code I have not broken.
Because she cannot speak, she has not spoken

except in tones for which there is no tongue,
except I sing the music she might have sung.

Now, at the end of century number twenty,
so many have plenty of nothing, I nothing of plenty.

Midway through my fifty-seventh year
she is not here.

You are shown
to the room
at the top of the stairs:

Number One, it says on the door.
And you have worked hard
to get here.

There is a sitting room
through which,
once you have wired

the window open
with a coat hanger,
a nice breeze blows.

The bath's across the hall:
the tub's quite functional, clean,
though with two faucets

the right toes boil, the left toes freeze.
Still, they will be washed.
There is no phone,

but none was expected.
Here most everyone drinks tea,
not coffee. The teapot also works.

Here they weigh your food in grams
and you in stones. My weight is stable:
I always weigh one stone.

In this many-windowed aerie
hot water is as slow to arrive as grace,
as the fifteenth century:

A minute, ten is the time to beat.
At the newsstand on High Street
there is the *Guardian*,

the (not the New York) *Times*,
the *Herald Tribune* that follows you
like a faithful dog.

You have flown all night
in order to walk the High this afternoon,
to have these drivers

aim at you good-naturedly
from the wrong side of the street.
But the biggest menace on the High

is the killer bicycle
that Oxford mounts each morning
dutifully like a mate.

Today is one day later
than when you left
your house three thousand miles away,

the dog boarded,
the rooms completely dark
except for the one light

left on for burglars.
You stroll these streets again
craning upward.

History hunches over you
like Toynbee, like time itself.
And in the mirror

in the WC, in the loo,
in the look on your face, haggard,
jet-lagged

you notice for the first time
the unmistakable features
of a gargoyle.

Still, Blackwells welcomes you.
You cross its bookish palm.
But just now

you are numb to words,
numb to numbers,
to the latest news from Bosnia,

Somalia, Northern Ireland.
In the famished whirl of time
you are swept up by friends

who have chosen Bangkok
though just for dinner.
The waitress glides

fro and to
exquisite porcelain
and brings you Coca-Cola

with a minimum of ice.
Otherwise the meal
three courses

is worthy of gods and goddesses
in and out of Thailand.
Leaving the restaurant, then,

staggered by the light
you wish the sun down
early over Oxford.

Before you go in search of bed, though,
you swerve right to pay your respects
to Shelley, laid out now one hundred years

on his granite slab, the Muse
mourning. You would kiss
her forehead, but she's still in jail.

And then, finally,
you find your room again.
Yes, quite functional. The curtains blow.

There is, thank God,
still no phone.
You close the curtains,

stretch out, right side
and immediately are asleep,
dreamless among the dreaming spires.

As it happens
you have come back here
on the shortest night

of any year. Yet when you wake
to bells and cars,
to the relentless Dopplered ambulance,

the zipping bicycles
silent as submarines,
when you wake further

to tea
and more tea
and then to breakfast

all around you
in this newest day of the world
in every corner of this city

in every paragraph
of the too thin *Herald Tribune*
in the grin of gargoyles—

everywhere you look around you,
there is increasing evidence
of what you might have least expected

here of all places
so far from home:
Home.

Piero Di Cosimo, ca. 1505
Ashmolean Museum, Oxford

Before the least
flame, before the blaze
transformed this glade into a pyre,
a prehistoric fear of fire
stalked the dark and days
of every beast

except the lion.
Swaggering like a king,
he may now be poised to learn
the lessons of beef and venison.
A possum and her young
are set to run.

Small birds discuss
the danger. They settle and surge.
The news is grave. Many will grieve.
Even the lioness turns to leave.
And from his perch, a large
black bird conducts.

The early smell
of burning has led some birds
to rise toward safety in the sky—
their mothers taught them how not to die,
though none of us know their words
for heaven or hell.

A human snout
floats in the face of a swine.
A bearded man-deer nudges his doe.
The herdsman driving his team must know
the truth: all are being
driven out.

Until today
this grove was most like Eden,
and then its trees began to glow,
and then, like God, Di Cosimo
conjured up a reason
to take it away.

from *The Lu Poems*

1. *Doorway*

Franz is beside himself
in the kitchen: dog dreams.
The door to my bedroom
is closed against the telephone

I lie on my side
trying for sleep

If I open my eyes
and look toward the door
I am for the moment afraid
I will see you there in the doorway

phosphorus in the darkness
in your newest clothes

I open my eyes
and for an eyeblink
only
one immortal second
you are there.

I lie down to sleep
beside myself.

2. Through the Window of the Cabin

at night
with my own ears
I heard the back and forth
of katydids
left, then *right,*
left, then *right*

like shuttle sounds
in the darkness
and so on into the night
left, then *right,*
until, then, *left*
and no answer

and, finally, *right.*

Then *left* and *right*
left and *right*
then *left* and no answer
left again
but no answer

until finally *right*
this time from a long way off
as though they were going away.

And they were.

3. Letter in the Form of a Poem

There having been
no further word from her
no sign

I package and send
her clothes on to you
Use what you can.

Send the rest
out into the breathless universe
of abandoned clothes

where all the bodied
or bodiless angels
may try them on

in the fullness of time
which will then close
around them

as simply and surely
as one might lower
a window.

Talking With The Mockingbird

The bird whistles up the evening
and so do I

then whistles it down
and I copy

mocking
the mockingbird.

When I twitter
the bird listens

and vice versa:
we are each the other's

audience of one.
Then, for fun, next time

the bird whistles
I keep quiet under the tree.

High up, impatiently,
the mocker trills again.

I follow then
in awkward playback

of his evening song.
The warbler pauses

as though I'd fashioned
a bogus tune

that might be true somewhere
but not in Georgia.

We listen again for each other,
I carefully for his lilting

hoping to hear a phrase or two
that just might make my night or day

a little sweeter: his tones are dulcet
as a flute, shrill as a jay.

Like Mozart in a master class,
he surrounds himself with newfound notes.

He seems to forget me then
in making music,

his own *ur*-song
by now long forgotten

or lost in some dazzling disguise.
He rests again—

to gather up, I want to think,
every blessèd one of his voices—

and flies.

Elegy and Affirmation

Together we are grateful, for we know
the privilege it is to touch another,
whether in the name of science or love.

The touching here has been made up of both.

By their extraordinary gifts
these dead have taught the living how to touch.

Through them we touch the body of the world.

Walking the Dog on the Night
Before He Is to Be Fixed

As far as I can tell, old chum, neuter
is neither here nor there, but in-between,
a state that has a certain charm, like pewter,
prized for durability, if not for sheen.

Tomorrow night you'll stroll in wary fashion
after the sleep, the knife, the careful scars
that promise to put an end to wayward passion
not to mention long-imagined wars

for territorial rights, a lady's paw.
Tomorrow the thermostat is set on cold
in calculated stern hormonal law.
What I know of this is what I'm told:

All veterans must come before the vet
on calendars either canine or lunar.
All lose that first fine frenzy to beget
whether it be later, friend, or sooner.

I toast us both then, Franz, in our decrease,
though there's no way for you to know that I'm
also tugging manfully at the leash,
waiting doggedly for the nick of time.

Canticles of Time

*libretto for choral symphony
in four movements*

I

Prologue

The mind remembers
what the tongue appreciates:
the bitter, sour, salt and sweet
of Time, its taste and texture
The mind savors. And celebrates.

II

Scio

For the great examination
all the generations gather

slate and notebook
chalk, eraser
blue books stacked up
on the desk

The brow furrows
and the fingers move

~

From these windows
we looked out
on the motions
of the world

In these rooms
we memorized
while around us
language swirled

in its many tongues:
vernacular of numbers
the dialects of joy
the grammar and the lexicon

of love

The who and what
where and when
the how and why
we know so much

and so little of

And then the bell, the bell
the last bell
It tolls for all
It tolls for you
The test is over,
the papers due.

III

Credo

To consider the lily
is to consider the rose

their perfect order

their breathing out
our breathing in

is to consider the heart
which keeps all standard time

To consider the rose
is to consider the lilac

their perfect fragrance

our breathing in
their breathing out

is to consider the heart
which keeps all timeless time

~

Mourn for those who are no longer here
whose chairs are empty
who sang their *gaudeamus igitur*
whose rest is silence

~

Meanwhile there is love
the elemental stone
Mercy, grace, and justice, too
But these are pseudonyms for love
These are love in its disguises

Thus we hope for love

Between our joy and grief
we know we do not know
nor do we understand
the alchemy by which
within the human heart

our hope becomes belief.

IV

Gaudeo

Blake was right: within our days
"Joy and Woe are woven fine"

Yet, of the faces we put on
the most enduring one is joy

Even the plainest word is praise:
I speak. Therefore I celebrate

And as each morning proves the world
so music proves the morning

Gaudeo. Gaudeamus.

music by Samuel Jones

Memory

is the ocean
in which she floats at random
touching or sometimes only trying

to touch those islands
of which she has always been
especially fond:

this one because it's the very one
on which her mother reigned
as the most beloved empress

this one
because it is the earth from which
she set adrift her husband's body

this one
because it's where
she hopes to move herself someday

away from wars and insistences
that she take her pills
to that calm latitude

where the camellias are forever gorgeous
and the pink crape myrtle
beautiful

beyond her present comprehension.

for Juanita Nelson

Transplant

The heart was harvested in Wisconsin
and flown in by helicopter.
    —*Atlanta radio news*

Within the green purpose of the room
there were ten beating hearts, but now are nine
who help the otherworldly pump assume
the flow of blood along the plastic line

by which the tenth now lives and has his being—
which is slow asleep, but dreams of moving,
of breathing on its own, of dimly seeing
its alien toes awake, all ten approving

the knitting of this widely opened chest—
where now there is no heart, but only pocket
until the circling mercy comes to rest
as neatly as an eye within its socket

and then the shock, the charmed expectant start,
the last astonished harvest of the heart.

While Watching His Own Echocardiogram
He Welcomes In the New Year

Bell that never bellowed
Hound without a bark
Fetus of my future
dancing in the dark

Nearest blood relation
Valentine alive
Great Somnambulation
toward which all engines strive

and Captain of the ferry
that charges me no fare:
May the New Year let you
win at solitaire.

Dear Tintinnabulation,
as new and wild bells ring,
Old Heart, Mortality,
how sweetly still you sing!

Singing from the West Coast

for Sarah Elias Stone

This Sunday morning
in San Francisco
you are at the epicenter

of whatever is to come.
Lately become your grandfather
I am in Atlanta

three hundred and fifty dollars away
talking by phone with your mother.
I can hear you in the background, singing,

holding forth in the living room.
I watch you with your mother's eyes:
you sway in your infant's

entertainment center, surrounded
by things that jingle
and drop to the floor.

You go absolutely nowhere.
You lollygag.
You play with your toes.

You croon and gurgle,
inventing the stories that you,
especially, will not remember.

Yesterday, for instance, while you
perched in your high chair
and gummed your Zwieback,

your mother offered you a smallish bribe:
"I'll give you ten dollars
if you'll say 'Ma-Ma' for me . . ."

at which you grinned
and promptly said "Da-Da!"
From the kitchen, your father cheered,

"That's Daddy's little girl, all right!"
That, I expect, is only one
of many such instances to come,

dear new and little one, in which you'll keep
both parents at once
precisely and so nicely off their balances.

Soon you will come east again, Sarah,
east to Georgia. There we'll bless you,
at least your toes, in the mountains,

in the cold endless waters of Big Creek,
to charm you back here often,
back and back.

This morning, though,
as you breathe and teethe
and celebrate,

the rest of the earth
is only part of the puzzle
you ponder, day to night:

The trickiest riddle of all, of course,
is yourself—and your toes
just ten small beginnings.

Now it's time for your breakfast.
After breakfast and perhaps a nap
and a year or two or five

there will come other feasts,
each in its own sweet time:
syllables, sentences, and schools,

flowers and weeds, poems and music
summers and hummingbirds,
languages and love—

all these and more
in the impatiences of time.
And let there always be time to sing,

as you do now,
over the humming distances
between us.

When I see you next, Sarah,
we'll sing together, we'll waste
glorious amounts of time,

we will lollygag in earnest.
And we'll never need to hurry,
you and I:

None of the banquets
of this world
would dare start

without you.

"Mosaics: Reflections from the Middle East"

In 1998, I joined a group that explored the Middle East, its history and ar-
chaeology. I was the sole physician, which figures in some of the poems.
Our itinerary included an amazing variety of sites, from the grand Roman
ruins of Baalbek, Lebanon, to the mountain that is commonly thought of
as Mount Sinai.

"Gaudeamus Igitur"

Gaudeamus Igitur was delivered as the Valediction Address at Emory
University School of Medicine in 1982. The Latin title is the first line of a
medieval song that became, over the centuries, a drinking song of cele-
bration in European universities. The Latin words of the first verse are
these:

Gaudeamus igitur,	*Post iucundam iuventutem,*
Iuvenes dum sumus;	*Post molestam senectutem,*
Gaudeamus igitur,	*Nos habebit humus,*
Iuvenes dum sumus;	*Nos habebit humus.*

The verse translates, roughly; "Therefore let us rejoice / While we are
young; / After a delightful youth, / After an irksome old age, / The grave
will contain us." The words and the tune to which they were sung have
special significance for an academic occasion such as Commencement:
Johannes Brahms later incorporated the song into the climactic portion
of his "Academic Festival Overture."

The form of the poem, in which every line begins with the word For, was
suggested by a portion of the long poem, *Jubilate Agno*, written by the
eighteenth-century poet Christopher Smart (1722–1771). The specific por-
tion referred to was written by Smart in praise of his cat Jeoffrey.

"The Forest Fire"

The painting, which hangs in the Ashmolean Museum in Oxford, is
mounted directly across the room from Ucello's *The Hunt by Night.* The
Ucello work is the subject of a notable poem by Derek Mahon, the con-
temporary Irish poet. When I visited the Ashmolean, I couldn't resist writ-

ing a poem to mirror Mahon's. *The Forest Fire* depicts an Eden-like scene about to be consumed by a huge fire. All the animals appear frightened except for the lion.

"Talking with the Mockingbird"

The mockingbird (mimus polyglottos) is a supreme student of music, but has always seemed a tragic figure to me. Although the bird rehearses endlessly the songs of all those he imitates, he seems to have forgotten his own first music, original and unique, as though the world's music had crowded in, demanding to be sung. Each of us learns first by mimicking our teachers. All the while, though, we are searching for our own unique voices. Helping us find that voice, it seems to me, is what good teachers help us do.

"Elegy and Affirmation"

This meditation was written for the annual Service of Gratitude and Reflection at Emory, in honor of those who donated their bodies to medical science.

"Canticles of Time"

In the late eighties, Millsaps College commissioned a choral symphony to be performed in 1990, its centennial year. The composer Samuel Jones, then at Rice University, was asked to write the music, I the words. Jones and I had been roommates at Millsaps, a fact that made the commission especially felicitous. As is customary, the words were to come first, then the music. I had trouble getting started until I found Latin titles to give the libretto a structure not unlike a mass. Following the Prologue, the section titles are *Scio*—"I know;" *Credo*—"I believe;" and *Gaudeo*—"I rejoice." The Latin phrase *gaudeamus igitur* means "Therefore, let us rejoice." (see above Note).